Warehouse Theatre Company's

Knock Down Ginger
by **Mark Norfolk**

Knock Down Ginger
was commissioned by the Warehouse Theatre Company
and the world premiere took place at the Warehouse Theatre
on 13 June 2003

Warehouse Theatre Company Regd. Charity No: 272816

Supported by
CROYDON
COUNCIL

Association of
London Government

Knock Down Ginger
by Mark Norfolk

Luke	Troy Glasgow
Nelson	Sylvester Williams
Charlie	William Maxwell
PC Chisholm	Darren Machin
Jenny	Judith Jacob

Directed by	Jeffery Kissoon
Designed by	Ellen Cairns
Lighting Designer	Matthew Eagland
Stage Manager	Denzel Williamson
Assistant Stage Manager	Alexandra Nunn
Production Manager	Graham Constable
Casting	Sooki McShane
National Press Agent	KWPR
Produced by	Evita Bier and Ted Craig

Troy Glasgow

Troy has recently graduated from The BRIT School and this is his first appearance in theatre. He began his television career appearing as Justin in the ground breaking drama *Out Of Control* (BBC). Since then, he has appeared as Denzil in *The Bill* (Thames); Bradley in *Kerching; Baby Father* and *Trail of Guilt* (all for BBC). He has also appeared in several pop videos, including those for David Gray, So Solid Crew and Asher D, as well as taking part in a video installation for the artist Mark Lewis.

Sylvester Williams

Sylvester trained at the Anna Scher theatre and has worked across all disciplines in a career spanning twenty-six years. He was most recently seen in the British Premiere of *Fruit Salad* at The Greenwich Theatre directed by Dawn Reid. Other notable theatre credits include the lead part of Ray in *Eden!* at The Theatre Royal Stratford East; *Black Poppies* at the RNT and a number of productions for the Black Theatre Co-operative. Sylvester is also a member of *The Posse*. On television Sylvester played the regular character of Mick McFarlane in *EastEnders* for five years and has also appeared in *Thief Takers* (Carlton); *Desmonds* (Humphrey Barclay for Channel 4); *Lytton's Diary* (Thames) to name a few. Film credits include: *Simple* directed by Michael Buffong and the role of Juka in *Sheena* (Columbia Pictures).

William Maxwell

Born in Liverpool, Bill started his career at Oldham. He then went on to work in Rep in Nottingham, Liverpool, Farnham, Colchester, Westcliff, Cardiff, Ipswich, and Canterbury. Tours include *Comedians* (Old Vic); Huntly-Pike in *A Chorus Of Disapproval*; Northumberland in *Richard I* and Hastings in *Richard III* all directed by Clifford Williams. He also played Macleish on tour with *The Long, The Short And The Tall*, Davies in Pinter's *The Caretaker* at the Ensemble Theatre in Vienna and he returned to appear in *The Dumb Waiter* and *An Ideal Husband*. Bill spent three years with the Royal Shakespeare Company including *Nicholas Nickleby* which was filmed and played on Broadway, as well as Sir Toby Belch in *Twelfth Night*, Vlok in *Jail Diary Of Albie*

Sachs, *Julius Caesar* and *Baal*. His most recent theatre credits include General Tilney in *Northanger Abbey* (Queen's Theatre, Hornchurch); Charles in *Me & My Girl* (Lincoln, Theatre Royal); *The Resistable Rise of Arturo Ui* (Manchester Library); Hugh in *Grace*; The Magistrate in *Lysistrata* and Scrooge in *A Christmas Carol* (all for The Steam Industry/BAC/Finborough). His latest appearance was as Willy Loman in *Death of a Salesman* (English Theatre of Frankfurt). Films include *Witchfinder General*, *William Tell* (directed by Mai Zetterling); *The Terence Davies Trilogy* and *The Ploughmans Lunch*, among others. Most recently *Brothers In Trouble* and the low budget feature *The Temple Project*. He has also recorded many radio plays for the BBC and LBC. Bill has appeared in numerous TV roles going back to leads in *X Cars* and *Softly Softly*, *King Of The Castle* (Willy Russell's first TV play) and *Six Wives Of Henry VIII*. Through the years he has featured in *Nearest and Dearest*, *The Dustbinmen* and countless other shows – including three separate characters in *Coronation Street* (Granada Television). He also played Yorkshire miners' President Jack Taylor in Channel 4's award winning *Strike of Our Time*. More recent credits include *Nothing Short of a Miracle*, *Bad Timing* and *Sunday Lunch*. Bill has also had several long periods playing Jack Sullivan (Terry's Dad) in *Brookside* (Mersey TV).

Darren Machin

Darren trained at the Webber Douglas Academy. Theatre credits include the No 1 tour of *Stand By Your Man*; two plays at the Mill at Sonning: *Worm's Eye View* and *Out of Order*; three plays at Keswick Century Theatre: *While the Sun Shines*, *Wait Until Dark*, *Run for Your Wife* four plays at the Palace Theatre Westcliff for Chris Dunham – *Straight and Narrow*, *Privates on Parade*, *Witness for the Prosecution*, *Girl's Night Out*. At Pitlochry Festival Theatre he was in *Lady Windermere's Fan* and *Sly Fox* for Clive Perry. He has also appeared in *Chorus of Disapproval* at the Wolsey Theatre in Ipswich, and in *Run for Your Wife* on tour and in the West End for Derek Nimmo. Television credits include *Family Affairs* and *Hollyoakes*.

Judith Jacob

Judith was born in London, and while still at school started working with the Anna Scher Theatre. Shortly afterwards she made her professional debut in *Jumping Bean Bag* (BBC). At the age of seventeen Judith played Nurse Beverly in the enormously popular television series *Angels* (BBC). Judith was a founding member of the Black Theatre Co-operative and, along with some other members, devised a programme which developed into the very popular ITV series *No Problem* (Channel 4). Other television credits include, Carmel in *Eastenders* (BBC); Miss Catchem in *Radio Roo* (BBC); a regular member of *The Real McCoy* team (BBC); Mrs Clarkson in *The Bill* (Thames TV); Mrs Coleman in *Dream Team* (Sky TV); Miss Kitts in *The Queen's Nose* (BBC); Sonia Davies in *Holby City* (BBC); *Victoria Wood as Seen on TV* (BBC); *Jackanory* (BBC); *Late Starter* (BBC); *Maids and the Mad Shooter* (BBC); *Maggie and Her Two People* and *The Gentle Touch* (all LWT). Judith made her Shakespearean debut playing what Irving Wardle of The Times described as 'an electrically mischievous Maria' in *Twelfth Night* at the Birmingham Rep. Other theatre credits include Sophonisba in *Waiting for Hannibal* (Black Theatre Co-op); Jean in *Meetings* (Black Theatre Co-op); Rap MC/Fairy in *Pinocchio* (Shaw); The BiBi Crew in *On a Level* (Stratford East) and Monica in *An Evening with Gary Lineker* (Hornchurch).

Mark Norfolk – Author

Mark Norfolk studied Speech and Drama at Middlesex University appearing on stage, TV and screen before working as a reporter and sports journalist. He has worked on documentary programmes for the BBC, Channel 4 and Sky Television before going to study Independent Film Production and avant garde Film Studies at University of Wales College, Cardiff. He has gone on to make a number of short films, which have been screened at film festivals around the world, and recently completed his debut feature *Love is Not Enough* which has received critical acclaim. His play about the Cato Street Conspiracy, *Fair As the Dark Get*, was short-listed for the 1998 Alfred Fagon Award. *Knock Down Ginger* is his third play and was also short-listed for the 2000 Verity Bargate Award which was recently work-shopped at the Soho Theatre and Writers Centre, where he was Writer in Attachment 2002.

Jeffery Kissoon – Director

Jeffery Kissoon's work in British theatre, film and television spans nearly three decades. He played Claudius and The Ghost in *Hamlet*, and Karna in the epic production of *The Mahabarata*, both directed by Peter Brook. Recent leads: Leko in Janet Suzman's South African version of Chekov's *The Cherry Orchard*, title role in *Macbeth*, and Prospero in Bill Alexander's production of *The Tempest* (Birmingham Rep); Brutus in David Thacker's RSC production of *Julius Caesar*, Oberon in Robert LePage's *A Midsummer Night's Dream* at the Royal National Theatre, Anthony in Yvonne Brewster/Talawa's production of *Antony and Cleopatra*, Odewale in Ola Rotimi's Nigerian version of *Oedipus*, the Singer in Theatre de Complicite's *Caucasian Chalk Circle* (RNT) and Basilio in Calderon's *Life is a Dream* (directed by Calixto Bieto at the Barbican, and Brooklyn Academy of Music). For the Glasgow Citizen's Theatre: *Tamburlaine, Oroonoko, The Three Penny Opera*, Jacques Roux in *Marat/Sade* and Goneril in *King Lear*. Jeffery appeared as Malcolm X in *The Meeting* (Warehouse Theatre, Greater London Authority Town Hall as part of Black History Month) and is currently playing Sultun Saladin in the highly acclaimed *Nathan the Wise* at Chichester Festival Theatre (directed by Steven Pimlott). Film & TV: Milton in *Eastenders, Holby City*, Steven Frears' *Dirty Pretty Things*, Branagh's *Hamlet*, Brook's *The Mahabharata, Space 1999, Grange Hill, Young Indiana Jones, Only Love, Brothers & Sisters, Dalziel And Pascoe, Z Cars*. As producer and director his work includes *Danny and the Deep Blue Sea, The Meeting* (1996); *Visions of Youth, Ave Africa, Knock Down Ginger* (director of Warehouse Theatre Writers In The Wings showcase 2002, Premio Candoni Arta Terme showcase 2002) and adapting and directing Ralph Ellison's *Invisible Man*.

Ellen Cairns – Designer

Ellen Cairns trained at Glasgow School of Art and The Slade. Her last collaboration with Ted Craig at the Warehouse Theatre was *Dick Barton: Flight Of The Phoenix* in 2002, having previously worked on *Happy and Glorious* in 1999. She designs extensively in this country and aboard. Recent credits include: the twenty-fifth anniversary production of *Educating Rita* (Liverpool Playhouse) updated by Willy Russell; *Les Miserables* and *Miss Saigon* in Estonia; Arthur Koestler's *Darkness at Noon* (Stockholm Stadsteater). She has also worked on *Moon on a Rainbow Shawl* for Nottingham Playhouse; *Bent* for Tallinn; *West Side Story* and an additional production of *Miss Saigon* for Helsinki.

Matthew Eagland – Lighting Designer

Previous work includes: *Darwin in Malibu* (Birmingham Rep); *Moon on a Rainbow Shawl* (Nottingham Playhouse); *Little Women* (The Novel Theatre Company at The Lillian Baylis Theatre); *Crossing Jerusalem, Ten Rounds, The Promise, A Night in November, The Wexford Trilogy* (*A Handful of Stars, Poor Beast in the Rain* and *Belfry*) (Tricycle); *A Taste of Honey, The Ghost Train,* and *Brief Encounter* (Queen's Theatre, Hornchurch); *Hay Fever* (Oxford Stage Company); *The Winter's Tale* for the Theatre Royal Bath as part of the Bath 2002 Shakespeare Festival; *The Arbitrary Adventures of an Accidental Terrorist* (NYT); *La Traviata* and *L'Elisir Di Amore* (English Touring Opera); *Tape* (New Venture Theatre, Brighton); *The Changeling* and *The Winter's Tale* (Southwark Playhouse); *An Evening with Gary Lineker, Bollywood 2000, Yet Another Love Story* and *Anna Christie* (Riverside Studios); *Belle* (The Gate); *Hamlet, The Winter's Tale, Confusions* and *The Pool Of Bethesda* (Guildhall School Of Music And Drama); *Tender Prayer* (Courtyard, Kings Cross); *The Age of Consent* (Pleasance, Edinburgh); *Moving On* (Bridewell Theatre); *Airport 2000* (Theatre Royal Stratford East at Greenwich Theatre); *Lark Rise* (Pegasus Theatre, Oxford); *Pericles* (Cochrane Theatre).

Denzel Williamson – Stage Manager

After starting at the BBC training as a floor manager, Denzel has since freelanced with companies such as Carib Theatre Co, Black Theatre Co (Nitro), Umoja, Black Mime, Double Edge, Talawa to name but a few. Denzel also has a passion for food, and now owns and jointly runs a Caribbean catering company: J.D Foodz – currently delighting the masses at 93 Feet East, 150 Brick Lane.

Alexandra Nunn – Assistant Stage Manager

Since graduating from the Courtyard Theatre Company, Alex has been involved in numerous productions in roles ranging from AM to Lighting Designer. Credits include: DSM/Operator *Sweeny Todd* (Bridewell Theatre); Touring Stage Manager *Envision* (The Moving World Theatre); ASM *Skin Deep* (Warehouse Theatre); Stage Manager *Big Boys* (Warehouse Theatre); Production Co-ordinator *The Meeting* (Warehouse Theatre); Assistant Stage Manager *Dick Barton Episode IV* (Warehouse Theatre); Stage Manager *Envision* (European tour) and Stage Manager *Antonio and Cleopatra* (Courtyard Theatre).

Graham Constable – Production Manager

Graham studied Stage Design and Performance at the Rijiksakademie, Amsterdam, and under Josef Szajkna at the Studio Theatre, Warsaw. He returned to London and formed ARC, a mixed media performance group. Graham has constructed settings and properties for film, television and theatre, for companies as diverse as BBC TV, Venezuelan TV, The Edinburgh Wax Museum and Glydebourne Opera. As the Warehouse Theatre's Production Manager, he has built over forty shows.

Founded in 1977 in one of Croydon's few remaining Victorian industrial buildings it soon built a national reputation for producing and presenting the best in new writing. In 1986 it launched the prestigious International Playwriting Festival. Having inaugurated a partnership with the leading Italian playwriting festival, the Premio Candoni-Arta Terme, in 1995, selected plays are now seen in Italy offering the potential for further performance opportunities in Europe. A partnership has also been formed with Theatro Ena in Cyprus. Previous winners such as Kevin Hood, whose play *Beached* won the first ever Festival, have gone on to achieve incredible success nationally and internationally. Kevin's two subsequent plays for the Warehouse, *The Astronomer's Garden* and *Sugar Hill Blues,* both transferred, the first to the Royal Court and the second to Hampstead Theatre. His most recent work includes the BBC2 series *In A Land Of Plenty.*

Today the Warehouse Theatre is acknowledged as one of the foremost theatres for new playwriting in the country. Other hugely successful productions have included *Sweet Phoebe,* by Australian playwright Michael Gow, which saw the London stage debut of Cate Blanchett, *Iona Rain* (winner of the 1995 International Playwriting Festival) and *The Blue Garden,* both by acclaimed playwright Peter Moffat and critically acclaimed *The Dove* by Bulgarian playwright Roumen Shomov. A continuing success is the company's stage version of *Dick Barton Special Agent.* First produced at the Warehouse in December 1998 it was an instant success, was brought back by popular demand in 1999 and then toured nationally. More success then followed with Episodes II, III and IV. Episode V has already been commissioned.

The theatre is also proud of its partnership with other companies who share the commitment to new work, discovering and promoting the fledgling Frantic Assembly and other companies like Red Shift, Theatre Alibi, Look Out Theatre and Hijinks. Long standing partnerships with Black Theatre Co-op (now Nitro) and Tara Arts has been in the forefront of the theatre's commitment to access and equality. It has a thriving youth group, a busy programme of multi-cultural work for young people and a Writers Workshop programme.

Warehouse Theatre Company

The Warehouse Theatre Company's International Playwrighting Festival
A National and International Stage for New Writing

Celebrating eighteen years of success, the IPF continues to discover and promote the work of new playwrights, consolidating the Warehouse Theatre's role as a powerhouse of new writing.

The IPF is held in two parts – plays from all over the world are entered into the competition and judged by a panel of distinguished theatre practitioners. The best selected plays are then showcased at the Festival weekend on 22 and 23 November.

Plays are also presented in Italy at the leading playwriting festival Premio Candoni Arta Terme and many selected plays go on to production in Britain and abroad. This year marks an eight year partnership with Premio Candoni Arta Terme and a year partnership with Theatro Ena, Nicosia.

Recent Successes

The Shagaround by Maggie Nevill, IPF 1999 selection, was the showcased in Italian at the Premio Candoni Arta Terme and at the Tricycle Theatre in English. The play, produced by the Warehouse Theatre Company and the Nuffield Theatre, Southampton has since toured at Nuffield Theatre (Southampton), Ashcroft Theatre (London), Soho Theatre (London) and Brighton Theatre Royal.

The Dove by Bulgarian playwright Roumen Shomov, IPF 1999 selection, was produced at the Warehouse Theatre in April–May 2000, was showcased at the Premio Candon Arta Terme the same year, and went on to be produced twice in Bulgaria.

> "This fascinating play by Roumen Shomov…an accurate reflection of the lunacy of daily life" *The Guardian*.

Real Estate by Richard Vincent, the IPF 1994 selection, was produced in Italy by II Centro per la Drammaturgia Contemporanea "H" and Beat 72 at Teatro Colosseo in Rome December 2001. Richard has received a commission to write a feature film from the UK Film Council and has recently been awarded a commission to write an episode of *Casualty* (BBC).

51 Peg by Phillip Edwards, the IPF 1998 selection, was showcased at the Premio Candoni Arta-Terme in Italy (May 1999) and was produced at the Edinburgh Festival 2000.

> "Edwards' script is exceptional…goes beyond the norm that most playwrights would find comfortable"
> *Edinburgh Evening News*

The *Resurrectionists* by Dominic McHale, the IPF 1997 selection, was premiered at the Warehouse Theatre in 1998, as a co-production between the Warehouse Theatre Company and the Octagon Theatre, Bolton. It was also performed at the Octagon the same year.

"Dominic McHale's entertaining debut...hilarious"
Evening Standard

Just Sitting by Andrew Shakeshaft, the IPF 2000 selection, premiered at Premio Candoni Arta-Terme 2001.

Knock Down Ginger by Mark Norfolk, the IPF 2001 selection was showcased as part of the Writers In The Wings (Warehouse Theatre 2002) and showcased at Premio Candoni Arta Terme (November 2002).

The selected plays for the International Playwriting Festival 2002 were *Paradiso* by Raymond Ramcharitar, *Black Other* by Dystin Johnson, *Blue Day* by Riou Benson, *A Scent of Lilac* by Lindy Newns and *Destroy Jim Hasselhoff* by Amy Jump.

The Dove

Sweet Phoebe

KNOCK DOWN GINGER

Mark Norfolk

KNOCK DOWN GINGER

OBERON BOOKS
LONDON

First published in 2003 by Oberon Books Ltd
521 Caledonian Road, London N7 9RH
Tel: +44 (0) 20 7607 3637 / Fax: +44 (0) 20 7607 3629
e-mail: info@oberonbooks.com
www.oberonbooks.com

A catalogue record for this book is available from the British
Library.

PB ISBN: 9781840023794
E ISBN: 9781786823298

Cover design by Jaded 2003

Characters

LUKE

NELSON

CHARLIE

CHISHOLM

JENNY

ACT ONE

Scene 1

A hard drum & bass hip hop music track pumps as lights fade up on a dowdy, working class living room of brown patterned carpet, beige wallpaper with tacky landscape prints on the wall. There's a well-worn, torn sofa, an armchair, a sideboard, and a table stacked high with newspapers. A television set has its back facing the audience. LUKE enters. He's a young black boy, aged about fifteen. He immediately goes to the sofa where he begins to search through its innards. His search is unsuccessful. He thinks for a moment before flicking on the television and a computer game. He plays silently, then ever more excitedly.

LUKE: (*Playing aggressively.*) Yeah, you're tryin' to fuck me! But y'know I'm bad! Yes…level three! Come again, Rasta!

The game starts a new level.

Liff it up selector! Level three a' gwan! MC Rockin' Luke in th' house tonight…all th' pretty girls dem outa' sight. So come bad bwoy MC, set th' house alight!

The doorbell rings.

Shit!

He plays less frenetically for a moment then increases his tempo.

The doorbell rings again.

No! I'm gonna fuck it up!

Another burst of ringing from the doorbell sends LUKE into a frenzy.

Oh, shit, man! Level fuckin' five…

LUKE exits, momentarily returning with NELSON, a hard black man, mid thirties. LUKE returns to his computer game.

LUKE: Gotta start again now.

NELSON moves to the window and peers out.

NELSON: You left me exposed out there, dread.

LUKE: I thought it was them kids.

NELSON: (*Pause.*) Boy, that Federale', Chisholm's on a raas mission, you knaa'.

LUKE: He had a go at me yesterday.

NELSON: Yeah?

LUKE: Bangin' on about you he was... (*The game.*) Ooh, yes!

NELSON: Sayin' what?

LUKE: Nothin'. Said he knows your gig.

NELSON: Fuck him. He don't know shit.

LUKE: He said he went school with you.

NELSON: We used to move together them times. Nothin' too tough. We were young, kids stuff. Fuckin' blue boy, I shoulda' known he was gonna follow in the family footsteps. What's that shit you're playin'?

LUKE: Deathwalker. I'm on level three. I got to level four earlier.

NELSON: All you youths love these kinda' fuckries, ennit.

LUKE: That's cos I'm a don. Watch me kill that thing there.

NELSON: Which t'ing?

LUKE: There there, that alien with the rocket launcher in his hand.

NELSON: That's a alien? That looks like somet'ing I leave in th' toilet…

LUKE: Na, na, it's a cellu-droid. You kinda' create it from a film at the beginnin', but I fucked it up.

NELSON: Still look like a piece o' shit. (*Beat.*) When's Charlie comin' back?

LUKE: Dunno. You're alright, man…

NELSON: I don't want him to catch me here.

LUKE: You're alright, man, he's with my mum. (*Distracted.*) Come on, man! Shit!

NELSON: You have to watch him, y' know.

LUKE: What, Charlie?

NELSON: Him same one.

LUKE: You're havin' a laugh, aint ya?

NELSON: He might go on soft, but the man's got history, y'get me.

LUKE: (*The game.*) Come on, come on…

NELSON: How come you're always round 'ere?

LUKE: He goes out with my mum sometimes, ennit.

NELSON: They gone out?

LUKE: Who? Dunno. Yeah, they gone down th' Socialist Workers…

NELSON: That place still goin'? I used to have a nice runnings down there with them teachers an' social workers. Them mans did hungry for that shit. (*Pause.*) I hear you give up your job?

LUKE: Not wrong. Don't have to get up early no more.

NELSON: That little paper round business was a nice little front… (*Beat.*) Hey, turn off that shit, I'm talkin' to you.

LUKE: Hold on, I'm kickin' arse…

Suddenly NELSON grabs the game.

NELSON: You think this is a joke business?

LUKE: I've never been on level five before.

NELSON tosses it to the floor.

LUKE: (*Pause.*) You're gonna break it. It aint even mine!

LUKE picks it up and checks it over.

NELSON: (*Indignantly.*) My father take licks to survive in this place, used to piss blood while the white man's inna nightclub drinkin' champagne from his money.

NELSON lightens his mood.

But eh, rude boy…for a youngster you're alright. I like the way you jus' drop in an' master this business still.

LUKE: Yeah…

NELSON: F'real, dread.

LUKE: (*Unsure.*) I just wanna get a bit o' money together, you know. Then I'm gonna…

NELSON: What?

LUKE: Gonna head out. Gonna get away. We're goin'.

NELSON: How you mean goin'? Things are cookin', man.

LUKE: I dunno. It's round here, ennit, it's borin'.

NELSON: It's excitement you want?

LUKE: An' that Dennis, bloke…

NELSON: Which Dennis?

LUKE: I hate him. Hate him.

NELSON: (*Realising.*) A man have to be master in his own house, y'get me.

LUKE: It aint his house.

NELSON: His woman, his house, you don't see it?

LUKE: No, I don't.

NELSON: You have a lot to learn.

LUKE: I don't know what she's doing with him anyway. He's a weedhead, man. He just sits around in his boxers all day. An' he's just on it…on it the whole time, weed, Special Brew. An' he smells. This smell just follows him round the house. She can do better than that. An' he hits her. Yeah, the other day, I come home an' she's there bawlin' her eyes out…

NELSON: She musta' done him somethin'…

LUKE: (*Exploding.*) He aint my dad, yeah. He aint my fuckin' dad!

NELSON: Hey, hey, hey, hol' it down, bredren, cool down. (*Pause.*) Hear what, I'll tell you what you do next time, yeah. Break a bottle, hold it up to his throat like this… make sure you draw blood. He'll know say it's no joke.

LUKE: (*Worried.*) I dunno…

NELSON: People will respect you.

LUKE: He's her man, though.

NELSON: This is not a personal thing.

LUKE: What about, I mean, she's my mum?

NELSON: Smarten up, dread! You want respect? I learn a long time ago that fear breeds respect. It don't just come to you, you have to earn it. Tchoh! I don't know why I bother with you young boys, you too soft. (*Beat.*) You ready to do this thing?

LUKE: Yeah.

NELSON: You sure you aint gonna pussy out on me?

LUKE: Yeah, no, I aint, I'm ready.

NELSON: You still have my thing?

LUKE: It's alright.

NELSON: It's alright?

LUKE: Yeah, it's safe, man.

NELSON: Good. That's just a little small something. But it's gonna do the business, set us up good. Hear what, this is no game for pussies, you get me. If you keep your head, you can make some proper dollars out there. We do it right, you an' me run this whole bomba claat place y'hear! Let's go.

Exit NELSON and LUKE.

Fade down lights.

Scene 2

Momentarily, two or three FIGURES enter with torches. They move round the room quietly, quickly, efficiently and begin to pull the room apart, tipping over the furniture, throwing things on the floor, all the while torch lights swishing round the room. There's a kind of symmetry to their action. After a short while they exit almost as quickly as they entered. Lights fade up on the living room in a terrible mess, there's obviously been a burglary. The table is overturned, the newspapers are scattered all about, the chairs and the side-board are overturned and various other items are strewn across the floor. Enter CHARLIE JOHNSON, an elderly man in his sixties, accompanied by a policeman. The officer shifts through the debris, vainly searching for clues. The officer is PC CHISHOLM, a large stocky man in his mid-late thirties. CHARLIE picks up a silver framed photograph from the floor which he stares at forlornly.

CHISHOLM: Don't touch anythin', not until after Socco dust the place down for prints. They'll be 'ere in about an hour.

CHARLIE: Forget it. They won't find much.

CHISHOLM: Tell you what though, they certainly made a mess of this place. Any ideas who may have done this, Mr Johnson?

CHARLIE: They killed her, you know…

CHISHOLM: Eh?

CHARLIE: No. Nothin'.

CHISHOLM: Anyone got a grudge against you?

CHARLIE: Grudge?

CHISHOLM: Yeah, you know, you fall out with someone an' they wanna make a point?

CHARLIE: Nothin' like that.

CHISHOLM: I know you, don't I?

CHARLIE: I know you.

CHISHOLM: Yeah?

CHARLIE: You're Ossie Chisholm's boy.

CHISHOLM: You know my dad?

CHARLIE: We went to the same school.

CHISHOLM: That so? Ever been in trouble… I mean, with the law?

CHARLIE: I'm the one's been burgled here.

CHISHOLM sifts through a pile of debris in a corner.

CHISHOLM: You got a son, haven't ya? Used to work this manor.

CHARLIE: He's an engineer now.

CHISHOLM: By all accounts he was a good copper. One of the best. Tipped for the top, so to speak.

CHARLIE: He loved his job.

CHISHOLM: But not enough to stay, eh. (*Pause.*) You say you can't see nothin' missin'?

CHARLIE: Not sure.

CHISHOLM: It's them scallys, that's what it is.

CHARLIE: It's a bloody game to them.

CHISHOLM: Sounds about right. That's their MO y'see. They watch ya, log your comings and goings. Then when you least expect it, they pounce, like a bunch o' bleedin' vultures.

CHARLIE: I aint got nothin'.

CHISHOLM: It's anythin' what they think they can sell. Down the market, car boot sale, door to door...

CHARLIE: The telly's gone.

CHISHOLM: Eh?

CHARLIE: The telly, it was over there.

CHISHOLM: Well, that's it then, y'see. (*Muttering.*) Little fuckers.

CHARLIE: What?

CHISHOLM: I'd love to get my hands on 'em.

They see Pensioners like yourself as fair game. It's a shame, this estate used to be a decent place to live in. Me an' the fellas down the nick are always goin' on about it. Now you got yer terrorism, yardies, car crime, its the manpower, y'see...

CHARLIE: (*Surveying the mess.*) Look at it, I gotta live here.

CHISHOLM: You got off lightly, mate. Sometimes them dirty bastards shit on the floor.

CHARLIE: Eh?

CHISHOLM: You got any jewellery or anythin' like that?

CHARLIE: Er, no.

CHISHOLM: Family heirlooms?

CHARLIE: No.

CHISHOLM: What about your missus, she got any – ?

CHARLIE: No, she, she died.

CHISHOLM: I'm sorry.

CHARLIE: She passed a year ago. It was our anniversary yesterday. I had a little do, a few drinks, you know, a commemoration.

CHISHOLM: (*Pause.*) You okay?

CHARLIE: Yeah, I'm fine.

CHISHOLM: Right, these kids, you ever see 'em, like, get a good look at 'em?

CHARLIE: By the time I get there they're long gone...

CHISHOLM: You musta' seen somethin'.

CHARLIE: I hear 'em, runnin', laughin'...

CHISHOLM: Yeah, I s'pose you're right. The art of the game is to knock and run.

CHARLIE: Yeah.

CHISHOLM pulls at some shabby clothing piled on the floor.

CHISHOLM: Hold on a minute, your TV...

CHARLIE: My TV?

CHISHOLM: Yeah, here it is, hidden under all this... Gor blimey, it's old, aint it. Is it colour?

CHARLIE: Millie, that's the wife, she used to bang on about gettin' a new one. But I didn't see the point if the old one still works.

CHISHOLM: Mr Johnson, is there anyone you can stay with for a few days, family, friends?

CHARLIE: I didn't go last time or the time before that.

CHISHOLM: It's getting worse round 'ere, you know. Maybe you ought to give it some thought.

CHARLIE: (*Stubbornly.*) I live here, this is my home.

CHISHOLM: I'm not the enemy here. I'm tryin' to help.

CHARLIE: I know. Sorry. I suppose you fancy a cuppa tea?

CHISHOLM: Tea? No, no thanks. Yeah, only last week in Gideon Road, this old dear wakes up in the middle of th' night to find some bloke standin' over her. I mean, she's terrified. But it turns out this nonce only wants to wear her clothes an' talk. I mean, what do you talk about wearin' old cardigans and a tweed skirt, eh?

Enter LUKE, carrying a bent bicycle wheel.

LUKE: What's goin' on?

CHISHOLM: (*Surprise.*) Well, well, look who it is! Like playin' games, do ya? Knock Down Ginger?

LUKE: That's a kid's game.

CHISHOLM: You that lary? Checkin' up on your victims now, eh?

LUKE: I come to see Charlie.

CHARLIE: Luke?

LUKE: The door was open.

CHISHOLM: Door open, was it?

LUKE: Yeah, it was wide open.

CHARLIE: What is it?

LUKE: I thought there might be trouble.

CHISHOLM: There's trouble alright. Take a good look. Take a good look at your handiwork...

CHISHOLM leads LUKE round the room.

LUKE: I aint done nothin'. This aint down to me!

CHISHOLM: That might well be the case. But what your mate hands out to them kids, he might just as well had come in here an' smashed the place up himself.

CHARLIE pulls LUKE away from the policeman.

CHARLIE: Get your hands off him. Go do your job!

CHISHOLM: This is my job! And he's up to no good, the little git. I've had my eye on him for some time.

CHARLIE: You should be out there stoppin' this lot from happenin'. But you waste your time harrassin' young kids!

CHISHOLM: It's these young kids what do all this! (*Checking himself.*) Er, alright, Mr Johnson, take it easy, calm down.

CHARLIE: Tell me to calm down! Every day I gotta walk round 'ere an' watch them animals shittin' on my doorstep. That's what killed her, that's what done it. Too scared to even take the dog for a walk she was. Frightened her to bloody death!

LUKE shakes the irate old man.

LUKE: Charlie, it's alright, it's alright. Why don't you go away an' leave us alone!

CHISHOLM: (*Pause.*) Right, I'll be off then. I reckon I'll go and catch some criminals.

CHISHOLM writes on his pad, tears the page out and hands it to CHARLIE.

CHISHOLM: You find anythin' missin', jus' pop down the station, or give us a call. You'll need a crime report number for the insurance…if you got any.

Exit CHISHOLM.

LUKE and CHARLIE silently try to put some semblance of order to the room.

CHARLIE spots LUKE rummaging around in a tear in the sofa.

CHARLIE: Oi, you're damagin' my settee!

LUKE: Look at it, it's already damaged.

They work together in unspoken harmony.

LUKE: (*Brightly.*) Nearly back to normal, eh?

CHARLIE: You think?

LUKE: I'm gonna find out who done this, and when I do…

CHARLIE: And what?

LUKE: Nothin'.

CHARLIE: You're gonna find out who done it?

LUKE: Yeah.

CHARLIE: And what?

LUKE: Creepers an' house breakers…nuff people hate them mans there. Sometimes they come in your yard when you're sleeping.

CHARLIE: And what?

LUKE: They teef your stuff, ennit?

CHARLIE: You're gonna find out who done this?

LUKE: Yeah, I am.

CHARLIE: And what?

LUKE: I dunno. Nothing.

CHARLIE laughs.

You'll have to wait an' see, won't ya?

CHARLIE: Think I was born yesterday?

CHARLIE walks slowly over to the window where he can see the sprawling estate outside.

It's funny if it were funny. That's what this place does to you. It's like that. You think you got it beat, but all the time it's got you licked. Then you're stuck. No choice. Wanna be here all your life?

LUKE: What, like you?

CHARLIE: I can still remember the old bottle-fillin' factory on the other side of town. Used to be buzzin' then. Over eighteen hundred blokes worked there. Used to be able to hear when the shift was over. Like a ship's foghorn it was. And when they come out, it was like watchin' a swarm of ants spread all over town.

'Course that's all gone now.(*Sighing.*) I'm a boy an' I say to my old man I wanna go university, he'd still be laughin' today as he clocks off his fifteen hour shift. You get opportunities now unthinkable back then.

LUKE bursts out laughing.

LUKE: Opportunities? What opportunities? Don't you read the papers?

CHARLIE: I read 'em.

LUKE: It's poverty, ennit. I saw it on telly the other day, it said crime is linked to poverty.

CHARLIE: Bullshit. It's alright for them woolies sittin' up there in their ivory towers tellin' us little people what's wrong with us down here. Don't you listen to that liberal crap, son.

LUKE: I read the papers, Charlie. I know what's goin' on round 'ere.

CHARLIE: You do, do ya?

LUKE: I see 'em out there every day, no job, no money, no chance. Can't even look after their family.

CHARLIE: They won't from a street corner.

LUKE: So what you sayin'?

CHARLIE: What I'm sayin' is, it don't have to be that way, Luke. Not today. Everyone's got a choice.

LUKE: What choice? That pisshead who's always hangin' about by the cashpoint machine, what choice has he got?

CHARLIE: He wants to stop drinkin' for a start.

LUKE: An' them refugees, them Kossovans selling fags on the corner, they're like…they're not even allowed to work or anythin'.

CHARLIE: Don't you worry about them, they're doin' better than you an' me.

LUKE: (*Beat.*) That's true, you know. They can't even speak the lingo but some of them got cars, bad trainers, the latest fashion, you get me.

CHARLIE: Education's what it's all about today, O Levels, A levels, degrees. If you stay on at school –

LUKE: (*Interrupting.*) Later to that! Man can earn nuff dollars without all that shit.

CHARLIE: You think?

LUKE: You jus' gotta be prepared to hustle.

CHARLIE: Hustle?

LUKE: Gotta work hard, get yourself a good runnings, ennit. All me now, it's bling, bling, struttin' in my yard, seven series drop-top park up on the drive, a Beemer… (*Beat.*) Nah, forget that, a Lex or a low profile Mercs… might even have all of them, blood.

CHARLIE: That aint the way, Luke.

LUKE: (*Laughing.*) Come on, Mr 'J', give us a break.

CHARLIE: All them out there got breaks, an' look at 'em.

LUKE: Fix up, Charlie, man.

CHARLIE: I got a son won't cross two words wi' me, no money, no pension to talk about… It'll be a cryin' shame to see you turn out that way. Break your mum's heart it will.

LUKE: Yeah, yeah, yeah, you finished now, yeah?

CHARLIE: She aint been too happy with you lately.

LUKE: Tell me somethin' I don't know.

CHARLIE: Round 'ere watchin' telly, playin' computer games…your lies are gonna land you in a pile o' shit.

LUKE: What lies? What you goin' on with?

CHARLIE: I was young once, y'know.

LUKE: Yeah, so what?

CHARLIE: So what?

LUKE: Yeah, so what?

CHARLIE: So you aint been bunkin' off school, then, eh?

LUKE: (*A little thrown.*) No, I aint.

CHARLIE: I aint as dumb as I look.

LUKE: You don't know nothing, mate. Goin' on like you know everything…

CHARLIE: If you had any sense, you'll see this as a warning.

LUKE: Well, you know what you can do with that.

CHARLIE: You know what your problem is? Your chatter, your big mouth.

LUKE: (*Peeved.*) What! Look, Charlie, you're an old geezer, right, an' it's only respect for your age why I'm even botherin' to listen to you!

CHARLIE reacts angrily, suddenly grabbing LUKE and getting him in a head-lock.

What you doin'? Let go, let go of me!

CHARLIE: You wanna take me on, do ya! What's got into you, this what you want?

LUKE: Gettoff me, man!

CHARLIE: Think you're smart, do ya? If I had a pound for every kid like you... all walkin' around 'ere with them mobile phones... go on, tell me what you want with a mobile phone?

LUKE: Get off, what's wrong with you? This is the twenty first century! Everyone's got mobiles.

LUKE reacts angrily, reaching into his pocket and taking out a mobile phone.

(*Testily.*) This what you want?

CHARLIE releases his grip on LUKE and straightens up, fixing his shirt.

CHARLIE: You know what that is? It's a line straight from hell sayin' go to jail...

The doorbell rings.

LUKE: Now you're properly finished.

LUKE plugs his computer game into the television and begins silently playing it.

There's a pause, then the doorbell rings again.

CHARLIE goes to the door, momentarily returning accompanied by JENNY, a thirty-three year old black woman, smartly dressed.

CHARLIE opens an envelope taking out a card.

CHARLIE:... I think back about what we coulda' done to change things an' that, but...

JENNY: There was nothin' no-one could do.

CHARLIE: Like the Blackwall Tunnel the doctor said. If somethin' breaks down in there the whole lot comes to a bloody standstill.

JENNY: A good woman, she was.

CHARLIE places the card on the mantle-piece.

CHARLIE: Thanks, Jenny.

JENNY: She was a good woman.

CHARLIE: Yeah, you don't expect it. I was readin' in the paper there, that if you get 'em early, they can cut 'em out. Good chance of making a full recovery then. There's so much I didn't say, you know, it's…

JENNY: Not fair is it. She was a good woman. Everyone loved her.

CHARLIE: (*Beat.*) You got this thing to go to, aint ya?

JENNY: Only goin' up the Mecca. I come to get him. Could stay a bit longer if you like?

CHARLIE: Nah, you go, I'll be alright.

JENNY: You ready then, Luke?

LUKE doesn't respond.

Luke!

LUKE: Nah, I'm stayin' here a bit.

CHARLIE: Go on son, off you go.

LUKE: I'm playin' computer.

JENNY: I told Dennis we'll meet him down the high street.

LUKE: I dunno…

JENNY: I thought it'd be nice, the three of us together.

LUKE: I'll meet you in there, won't I.

JENNY: I thought we'd go to McDonald's first.

LUKE: Not hungry.

JENNY: (*Exasperated.*) Luke!

LUKE: I had somethin' to eat already. I had a sandwich, didn't I Charlie?

CHARLIE shrugs.

JENNY: He aint gonna be happy.

LUKE: (*Equally exasperated.*) Mum!

JENNY: Don't you 'Mum' me!

LUKE: Mum!

JENNY: See what I have to deal with, Charlie, the boy's so feisty! I should give him a slap.

LUKE: I don't think so!

JENNY: (*Jovially.*) Nex' time I give you a slap upside your head!

LUKE: Yeah, right, whatever!

JENNY gives LUKE a playful slap.

JENNY: (*Mimicking.*) Yeah, right, whatever!

LUKE: Mum!

JENNY: (*Mocking.*) Mum! Y'see, I'm your mother. Alright then, Charlie. Sure you're alright? I got me mobile, I can phone Dennis, tell him we'll meet him later?

CHARLIE: Nah, you go on an' enjoy yourself.

JENNY: (*To LUKE.*) Oi, you, it shuts at ten.

Exit JENNY .

LUKE continues playing the computer game.

There's a pause.

CHARLIE: One good thing about today...

The doorbell rings.

Aah, well…

LUKE: Today, again? They got no respect, man.

The doorbell rings again.

LUKE is frantic as he struggles to concentrate on the game.

Shit! Don't it bother you?

CHARLIE: Ya get used to it.

LUKE: It's doin' my head in. I was on level four!

LUKE aggressively abandons the computer game and exits the room.

There is a commotion at the door, shouting and hollering.

(*Off.*) Oi, come here! I see ya! I know who it is. I'll get you next time, believe!

Enter LUKE.

CHARLIE: Who is it, you see them?

LUKE: I'm positive it's that Dundus an' his little mates, y'know.

CHARLIE: Who?

LUKE: Y'know, the little ginger with them freckles all over his face.

CHARLIE: Black kid?

LUKE: That's what they call 'em in Jamaica… Dundus.

CHARLIE: Well, in England, I believe the kid's name is Troy.

LUKE: He's rude, y'know. Last week he tried to sell me a car radio – he's only eight.

CHARLIE: Bloody kids.

There's a pause.

LUKE: So what about the 'do' yesterday?

CHARLIE: Nice of everyone to come.

LUKE: Your Alex didn't stay long.

CHARLIE: He never much liked it round 'ere.

LUKE: He's a well serious geezer though, ennit.

CHARLIE: Loved his mum.

LUKE: Come all this way on his jack, acting like a right wanker.

CHARLIE: I thought with Millie gone, he might... oh, I don't know.

LUKE: You shoulda' had a word, mate.

CHARLIE: Waste of time.

LUKE: He was screwing, you get me.

CHARLIE: Oh, he's a nice enough bloke.

LUKE: I thought he was gonna be having up geezers in the party. Then he just left.

CHARLIE: S'pect he had to dash off. It's some trek out to where he lives.

LUKE: All them people turn up, he was only 'ere ten minutes! That was a proper diss, trust me.

CHARLIE: He's grown up, he can do what he wants.

LUKE: I wouldn't diss my dad like that. There's something about him, man. He was goin' on like 'Five O', blood. He was just eyeing up everybody, believe.

There's a pause.

LUKE: What about the spread, then eh? All that ham an' cheese an' tuna. That's what you like, ennit? Yeah, you love that tuna. But that was it, man, she had buggerall money.

CHARLIE: Mind yer language.

LUKE: What? Bugger aint swearin'.

CHARLIE: It is in my book.

LUKE: It's what you say when you don't wanna say f –

CHARLIE: You windin' me up?

LUKE: No. I was jus' sayin' you're lucky.

CHARLIE: Oh yeah?

LUKE: Got no dough, has she. She's bruk, brassic.

CHARLIE: What about whatsisname?

LUKE: (*Sneering.*) Him?

CHARLIE: You take the time to talk to him you might find he's alright.

LUKE: I don't think so. She's mad hangin' about with a loser like that. He aint got jack. He's the living ponce. All he wants is – (*Pause.*) Anyway, your sarnies were down to me. I give her the money.

CHARLIE: An' you want it back.

LUKE: No, no, I was jus' sayin' that I give her the money to get the sandwiches.

CHARLIE: You want it back then?

LUKE: No, I was just sayin'… oh, bugger it.

CHARLIE: Language. (*Beat.*) So, you're flush?

LUKE: Eh?

CHARLIE: Got money to give away?

LUKE: What money?

CHARLIE: You spent the last half hour tellin' me how you give away your money to buy my sandwiches.

LUKE: Eh? No, I'm stocktakin' for Khan, ennit.

CHARLIE: Mister Kahn to you.

LUKE: I mean, he's only givin' me a fiver.

CHARLIE: On top of your paper round, must add up to a tidy sum.

LUKE: What's my name! I'm gonna earn real money, man…move away from this dump –

CHARLIE: You're fourteen, slow down.

LUKE: Fifteen actually, nearly sixteen!

CHARLIE: You concentrate on gettin' some O Levels. Give yourself a chance out there –

LUKE: Leave it out, Mr 'J'! (*Beat.*) Tchoh! I'm gonna kick some computer arse.

LUKE turns on the television and picks up his computer game.

CHARLIE: (*Pause.*) Oi, I thought you was workin'?

LUKE: Uh?

CHARLIE: You said you was workin'?

LUKE: Yeah…

CHARLIE: So what about this mornin' then?

LUKE: Do what?

CHARLIE: This mornin'.

LUKE: When?

CHARLIE: This mornin' I went for my paper an' I bumped into Mr Kahn…

LUKE: So?

CHARLIE: Had one of them bags over his shoulder. Doin' your work he was. What, you forget to wake up?

LUKE: Aint mine no more.

CHARLIE: What's that?

LUKE: Jacked it in, mate.

CHARLIE: You what?

LUKE: Too much stress, man.

CHARLIE: Stress?

LUKE: All that naggin', 'Don't be late, you ripped this paper, walked 'cross that garden.' He don't pay me enough for that.

CHARLIE: Right little big man, aint ya?

LUKE: No. I was doin' him a favour.

CHARLIE: You an' your big ideas.

LUKE: No.

CHARLIE: Five-thirty he's up every day to sort them papers –

LUKE: (*Facetiously.*) He'll have to post them as well now.

CHARLIE: Discipline, that is.

LUKE: He'll get someone else, won't he.

CHARLIE: Round 'ere?

LUKE: There's plenty geezers wanna earn a side money.

CHARLIE: You can't trust half the bleeders. Have it away with the till soon as look at 'em.

LUKE: Aint no money in that till.

CHARLIE: When I was a boy I used to be down the stables for half-four of a mornin' before school.

LUKE: Stables?

CHARLIE: Used to help on th' milk round – we had horses in those days.

LUKE: Horses?

CHARLIE: Had to wash 'em, feed 'em an' saddle 'em. Cor, you kids got it easy these days.

LUKE: Horses, that's funny, man. (*Beat.*) I Dunno, Mr 'J', I'll have to think about it.

CHARLIE: Might consider doin' it meself.

LUKE: Yeah, right.

CHARLIE: Money's money.

LUKE: I'm gonna be late.

LUKE turns off the television and picks up his bent bicycle wheel.

Tchoh, man, look at that! Thirty quid that's gonna cost me. I come off the pavement, didn't I...smacked into this motor. It belonged to this hard-core geezer in a wicked beemer. I mean it was just a little scratch, but he was well vex.

CHARLIE: How many times have I told you pavements is for walkin' on.

LUKE: (*Continuing.*) I mean, I clipped his bumper... thought I was down for a slap for sure.

CHARLIE: No doubt deserved one.

LUKE: His car is th' lick, Charlie, man. It's metallic black, got them little silver bits in the paintwork. An' it's got these windows... wicked. They're like sunglasses... you know when the sun comes out, they kinda block it out, that ultra violet an' shit. It's bad, man!

CHARLIE: Live round 'ere, does he?

LUKE: I seen his car about. It used to drive past... I used to say, 'Love that!'

CHARLIE: Sounds like trouble.

LUKE: (*Testily.*) How do you know?

CHARLIE: You hear what I say, an' keep clear.

LUKE: You weren't even there.

CHARLIE: Stay away.

LUKE: You don't even know what he looks like.

CHARLIE: I know his family.

LUKE: You think you know everyone.

CHARLIE: I knew his old man. Mean looking fella he was, pretty good fighter in his day. But he lost it when he got in with the wrong crowd. Poor bastard went mad.

LUKE: He went mad?

CHARLIE: Mad.

LUKE: What, like mad mad?

CHARLIE: Mad mad. Loopy, doolally. Used to be shoutin' at cars on the high street.

LUKE: Yeah?

CHARLIE: See him sometimes, he wouldn't even recognise ya.

LUKE: (*Laughing.*) No. What's all that about?

CHARLIE: No rhyme or reason.

LUKE: They should be locked up.

CHARLIE: Well, that's exactly what they did. Electric shock treatment, the works. I went up there one day, cryin' like a baby, he was. He used to cry in the ring when he won, which weren't that often. Black Cockerel they called him, on account of the way he used to strut round like one of them cocks at a cockfight. He was in a right state, what with the drugs, shakin', dribblin'… Poor bastard. Him what you're talkin' about, that's his son.

LUKE: Shit, man, you do know everyone.

CHARLIE: I jus' keeps meself to meself an' my eyes open. Aint you goin' somewhere?

LUKE: Nah, can't be bothered now. I'll give it a miss.

CHARLIE: You were off a minute ago?

LUKE: I'll go tomorrow, won't I?

CHARLIE: God, you're an unreliable bugger.

LUKE: There you go, you said it again.

CHARLIE: I'll say you again in a minute, unreliable so and so. While you're here, I got a letter come today.

LUKE gets a bunch of letters from the mantelpiece and sifts through them quickly.

LUKE: It's only a statement.

CHARLIE: It come first thing.

LUKE: The rest is junk mail.

CHARLIE: Alright is it?

LUKE: Yeah, it just tells you what's been paid.

CHARLIE: Don't want you walkin' out that door and a bunch of baillifs turn up.

LUKE: (*Self-satisfied.*) Do you get any more bills from the taxman?

CHARLIE: We'll see, won't we?

LUKE: An' the TV Licence people?

CHARLIE: That was then.

LUKE: The bank?

CHARLIE: It don't mean they won't send out any more bills from their bloody computer.

LUKE: Charlie, man, trust me. I bet in your day you never even knew what a computer was?

CHARLIE: Yeah, that's right, clever clogs. What's eleven twelves?

LUKE: What?

CHARLIE: Eleven times twelve, come on.

LUKE: Eleven times twelve, I know that…

CHARLIE: What is it then, come on Einstein?

LUKE: Gimme time…

CHARLIE: Eleven elevens: hundred an' twenty one, twelve twelves: hundred an' forty four, thirteen thirteens: hundred an' sixty nine. You lot bring calculators into exams. You're bloody buggered if the batteries are flat.

LUKE: You said buggered!

CHARLIE: I can.

LUKE: That's so not fair.

CHARLIE: Who pays the rent?

LUKE: The council.

CHARLIE: Go on with ya! (*Doleful.*) Computers, tax, bank...my Millie used to take care of all that stuff. Now she's gone. Nothin' ever stays sensible, Luke, you remember that.

LUKE: Don't worry, Charlie, you're alright as long as I'm around.

The doorbell rings.

CHARLIE: Bailiffs are early.

LUKE: It's them stupid kids again...

The doorbell rings again.

LUKE: That's it! I'm gonna give 'em a right kickin'!

CHARLIE: You sit down there, you idiot. I'll go.

LUKE: Idiot? Coffin dodger...

CHARLIE: What was that?

LUKE: What?

CHARLIE: I heard ya.

LUKE: I never said nothin', Charlie.

Exit CHARLIE.

LUKE returns to his computer game.

Enter CHARLIE with NELSON.

NELSON: Yeah, sorry to bust in on you like this...

CHARLIE: Luke...

LUKE stops playing the computer game.

NELSON: Alright, spar?

LUKE: Yeah.

NELSON struts the room.

NELSON: Yeah, yeah…jus' wanna show respect, yeah…
you know how it stay when a black man's got anythin'.
Tchoh! That Chisholm's a bad man, you knaa'. He goes
on a way, true he thinks he knows what's on street.
(*Singing.*) 'Heed my words wicked man
With your finger on the trigger of the gun
But he's a Babylon
An' I an' I day will come
Ooh, yeah…'

CHARLIE: Horatio, what you up to these days?

NELSON: Boy, this an' that you know, Charlie.

CHARLIE: Looks like you're doin' alright.

NELSON: (*Indicating his colour.*) That's a tough one when
you got this, y' knaa'.

CHARLIE: Oh yeah?

NELSON: F'real. It's all about the duckin', the divin' an'
the skivin', you get me.

CHARLIE: That so? What age're you now, thirty-eight,
forty?

NELSON: (*Laughing.*) Yeah, yeah, true you always been
a joker, Charlie. (*Short pause.*) Hear what, they don't
call me that no more, you know, that Horatio business.
They don't call me by that name no more.

CHARLIE: That's your name, aint it?

NELSON: True that's the name my father give me, kinda'
slave name an' t'ing.

CHARLIE: An' you aint a slave no more.

NELSON: I do my own t'ing, y'know. Master o' my own destiny, you get me.

CHARLIE: So what you called then?

LUKE and NELSON speak together.

LUKE / NELSON: Nelson.

They touch fists.

NELSON: Respect, Rudeboy.

CHARLIE: Nelson. Call yourself after one of the world's great statesman, eh?

NELSON: Yeah, that's what I thought, like, you get me. He was a leader, dread!

CHARLIE: Yes, he was certainly a game bloke. Not many could handle what he went through.

NELSON: For real.

CHARLIE: Twenty odd years of jail, an' no malice when he come out. That's greatness that is, the mark of a great man.

NELSON: (*Pause.*) He never went prison.

CHARLIE: Eh?

NELSON: Them kinda' people don't know nothin' 'bout jail.

CHARLIE: He was in jail. Everyone knows that.

NELSON: (*To LUKE.*) Whatsamatter with him? Charlie, man, the man never went to no jail. I read books on the bredder an' they don't mention jail in none o' them. An' I'm talkin' way back from when I went school.

CHARLIE: So you're sayin' he never spent twenty odd years in jail?

NELSON: No, blood.

CHARLIE: He wasn't in solitary for twenty-seven years?

NELSON: Never.

CHARLIE: So all that stuff about him is all lies?

NELSON: I don't know who tell you all that. They musta' been takin' the big piss. How come you don't know your own history?

CHARLIE: I know my history.

NELSON: Look how I have to tell a English man his own history. He was a sailor, Charlie…Admiral in the Royal Navy. 'England expects every man to do his duty…' an' t'ing an t'ing…

LUKE laughs.

CHARLIE: Oh, Lord Horatio Nelson.

NELSON: Yeah, he was a bad man, y' knaa. Waterloo an' all that. True he gave that Napoleon some wicked destruction, you get me. Go up Trafalgar Square an' all that, that's his place, rasta. Yeah… they dead him off an' he still there, y' know. Stannin' up there bold as brass. (*Beat.*) I heard he was a black man, y' knaa'? Yeah, yeah man. True you know how white man stay already – don't wanna acknowledge a black man history – But yeah… yeah, he was a black man, rude boy. He was dread, man. He was slammin' some bird up at Greenwich, there. They made a film about it – put a white actor in the part, but you know how it stay – it's only black man do them t'ings. That woman give up everything for him, an' she was married, you get me. (*Beat.*) Yeah, he was a black man for true, bredren. White man tek weh th' man history. (*Beat.*) I can't stop, you know, I'm on a t'ing. But hey, Rudeboy…

NELSON moves towards LUKE and gives him a hug.

LUKE is somewhat embarrassed as they shake hands.

Yeah, respect, nuff respect. If it wasn't for you, I'd be down th' station house, right now. (*Leaving.*) Listen, bredrens, I'm gone, yeah! Charlie, true you know you is a safe man, y' know, still. My ol' man tell me how you did look after him when he was in some scrapes them times. Hey, little man…

Exit NELSON.

LUKE stands and takes a hold of a pile of newspapers on the table.

LUKE: Want me to get rid of these?

CHARLIE: Aint finished reading 'em.

LUKE: It'll take you at least a year to get through them.

CHARLIE: It'll take as long as it takes.

LUKE: Your yard's gonna look like a doss house.

CHARLIE: You leave them be.

LUKE: Alright, alright.

CHARLIE: (*Beat.*) I'm an idiot, right?

LUKE: What?

CHARLIE: You heard. I'm sure of it, I've gone right soft in th' head.

LUKE: You on somethin'?

CHARLIE: So, go on, tell me…

LUKE: Tell you what?

CHARLIE: Do I look like a mug?

LUKE: (*Bemused.*) I don't know what you're on about.

CHARLIE: So c'mon, what's goin on?

LUKE: Nothing's goin' on?

CHARLIE: You gonna stand there an' lie to my face?

LUKE: No.

CHARLIE: Then what is it… between you an' him?

LUKE: Nothin'…

CHARLIE: Is that nothin goin' on, or nothin' between you an' him?

LUKE: Nothin'.

CHARLIE: Don't make me have to…

LUKE: (*Cutting in.*) He shoved this thing in my hand.

CHARLIE: He did what?

LUKE: I was holdin' onto it for him.

CHARLIE: You what?

LUKE: I swear, I don't even know what it is.

CHARLIE: You don't know what it is? It's you that's stupid.

LUKE: (*Agitated.*) There was nothin' I could do.

CHARLIE: (*Dismayed.*) Jesus Christ, have you any idea? D'you know…? Look, son…

LUKE: (*Interrupting.*) I told you, I bumped into his car an' he drapesed me up. I thought he was gonna hit me, then these two coppers turned up an' he put this thing in my hand.

CHARLIE: An' you didn't think to…?

LUKE: I was scared.

CHARLIE: You bring it round 'ere?

LUKE: I forgot I had it on me.

CHARLIE: You forget – now you're takin' the piss.

LUKE: I aint!

CHARLIE: Pisstaker.

LUKE: Why don't you believe me, I'm tellin' the truth. The police let me go, I went home, the thing was in my pocket. I forgot all about it.

CHARLIE: (*Beat.*) Get arrested?

LUKE: No.

CHARLIE: More's the pity.

LUKE: They jus' laughed at me.

CHARLIE: Ought to do their bloody job. What was it he give ya, that Lord Horatio Nelson…bloody cheek?

LUKE: I don't know. It was some packet, a little packet.

CHARLIE: Not that, just now.

LUKE: That was it.

CHARLIE: He didn't give you somethin' else?

LUKE: (*Frustrated and tearful.*) Why're you on at me? The fuckin' bloke aint give me nothin'!

CHARLIE: Don't you swear at me.

LUKE: You're makin' me.

CHARLIE: From what you're sayin', you saved him from doin' hard time. Check your pockets.

LUKE: I'm goin, man, you're trippin'.

CHARLIE: (*Sternly.*) Check your pockets!

LUKE: An' then I'm goin. I didn't come round 'ere to get abuse –

LUKE dips into his pockets and finds a folded note.

CHARLIE: Merry Christmas and Happy New Year.

LUKE: (*Shocked.*) Fifty pounds!

CHARLIE: I was hopin' this was a freebie.

LUKE: I gotta give it back, do I?

CHARLIE: He won't take it.

LUKE: (*Excitedly.*) I can get me a new wheel. An' if I do a deal...there's this bike shop near the butchers, the geezer in there, he's safe, man... I'm sure he'll do me a two for one.

CHARLIE: Stay away from him.

LUKE: Alright, Charlie, I aint stupid.

CHARLIE: Coulda' fooled me.

LUKE: Relax, man.

CHARLIE: His dad, Archie, was a bit simple, but at least he was an honourable man. Horatio, now he's a different kettle of fish, the worst kind. Before long, kid like you, he'll have tied up, wrapped up an' hung out to dry before you know what hit ya. Hook, line and bloody sinker. So if I was you I'd get down the nick. I got their phone number here...

LUKE: What you goin' on with? Grass? What am I talkin' to you for, what do you know?

CHARLIE: What do I know? I used to be a right toe-rag, myself, into allsorts. Even bought into a club with three other fellas, real hard nuts, spent most of our time dodgin' the old bill. So what happens to me one day? I wakes up with a conscience, pulled outa' the whole scam. Eventually it comes on top, an' I'm public enemy number one. The only thing saved my bacon was this.

(*Indicating his head.*) I arranged for police files to go missin' from the local nick and kept them. That's what guaranteed my safety, kept me alive. I've seen it, done it an' I own the T-shirt. An' believe me, it aint pretty. So you better listen to me when I tell you…

LUKE: Yeah, yeah, yeah, I'm gone.

Exit LUKE.

CHARLIE: (*Calling after.*) Luke, Luke! (*Pause.*) Crazy, crazy…this day an' age, you think by now they'd at least have some common sense.

CHARLIE makes his way over to the sideboard which he shifts a little to one side. He lifts up the carpet, exposing the floorboards. He then lifts up a small section of floorboard and reaches down into the floor where he pulls out a tied mass of paperwork. He opens the papers, flicking through the pages before finding what he's looking for. He then reaches for a telephone and carefully dials a number.

(*On telephone.*) Hello, Duke? Duke Fraser? He aint there? Is this eight seven two…? (*Beat.*) Oh, seven three? Sorry, don't know what happened there. Eyes aint as good as they used to be. (*Replacing receiver.*) Miserable cow.

He dials again.

Duke Fraser? It's Charlie, Charlie Johnson. That's right, Charlie Johnson. (*Beat.*) Yeah, it has been a long time, aint it. (*Beat.*) Look, Duke, I know you're probably a busy man, so I'll get straight to the point…

The doorbell rings.

Er, yeah, it's about four men, a boxin' match an' some missin' papers… (*Beat.*) You still there?

The doorbell rings again.

JENNY: (*Off.*) Charlie… Charlie, you in there?

CHARLIE looks round, thrown, suddenly nervous.

CHARLIE: Er, Duke, look, something's come up, can I call you back…? Yeah, 'course I will, one minute. G'bye.

He hangs up the receiver and replaces the paperwork in its hiding place.

The doorbell rings again.

JENNY: (*Off.*) Charlie!

CHARLIE: Alright, alright, I'm comin'.

CHARLIE exits, momentarily returning with JENNY.

What is it? You alright – ?

JENNY doesn't answer, her distress is obvious.

I'll put the kettle on.

CHARLIE moves towards the kitchen. JENNY follows.

You're done early?

JENNY: Changed me mind, didn't I.

CHARLIE: Where's erm…?

JENNY stops CHARLIE with a terse wave of the hand.

Oh?

There's an uncomfortable pause.

CHARLIE is slightly anxious as he moves back towards the living room area. He moves towards the telephone and lifts the receiver. But he changes his mind.

JENNY appears. There's another uneasy pause.

JENNY: There I was, standin' there like a lemon…

CHARLIE: What?

JENNY: I aint waitin' for him to come up with some lame excuse. He's takin' the piss outa' me, he is. I've had enough of it. He thinks I don't know he's been hangin' round after that slapper from the hairdressers.

CHARLIE: Rumours, Jenny.

JENNY: Everybody knows, Charlie. I've seen him sniffing round her myself.

CHARLIE: She's married, aint she?

JENNY: You wanna tell her that. Her man's supposed to be some mechanic...he needs to stop checking under cars an' start checking under his missus.

CHARLIE: (*Laughing.*) Jenny...

JENNY: Na, it's true. Excuse my French, Charlie, but the fat bastard really winds me up. (*Beat.*) Luke...?

CHARLIE: You jus' missed him. Left about five minutes ago.

JENNY: (*Remembering.*) Oh, we were gonna meet down McDonalds, weren't we? Oh shit, he's probably there now. (*Sighing.*) I worry about him, you know, Charlie.

CHARLIE: What, Luke?

JENNY: I do, I worry about him.

CHARLIE: What's botherin' ya?

JENNY: I dunno, Charlie. It's not like before, it's different. He's just... I never get to see him anymore...you know, talk to him, find out what he likes, don't like. It's just not like before. He goes on tough, like he's a man but he's just a boy really. An' I'm his mother, I brought him up, I should know about him. But I don't. I try, we do try, me an' Dennis, but it always just ends up in a shouting match...

I mean, I can't say nothin' to him. It's like, am I a bad mum? I dunno…

CHARLIE: Don't put yourself down, girl. There's plenty round 'ere be glad to do that for ya.

JENNY: I coulda' been a bloody nurse if I never got pregnant. I always wanted to be a nurse, you know, a nursery nurse. I loved kids. Even done a year at college studying for my certificate. That was before I moved here.

CHARLIE: (*Pause.*) You ever hear from him, Luke's dad?

JENNY: (*Sneering.*) Him! My mum warned me, said he was good-for-nothin'.

CHARLIE: They don't know whether they're comin' or goin', left, right or up an' down, young lads today.

JENNY: My friend swear she see him over the river – Sharee, she's got family over there – a couple of weeks ago, it was. I should set the CSA on his arse, they been hunting him down for ages.

CHARLIE: You wanna go to all that trouble, do ya?

JENNY: It's the principle, Charlie. The man should support his child. He's got no self-respect… Waster man. (*Beat.*) You know what I could do with right now? A good drink. Fancy one down the social?

CHARLIE: Nah, not tonight.

JENNY: Go on…

CHARLIE: No, gotta finish cleaning up after them kids.

JENNY: What kids?

CHARLIE: From the break-in.

JENNY: Break-in? What break-in?

CHARLIE: Well, sort of.

JENNY: Here? (*Beat.*) You can't stay 'ere then.

CHARLIE: I'm alright.

JENNY: No, no, s'pose they break in while you're here, can you imagine? No, you're comin' back to ours.

CHARLIE: Oh, Jenn, I'll be alright, it's jus' kids muckin' about.

JENNY: The same kids who been robbin' left, right an' centre.

CHARLIE: Police said it's just intimidation...

JENNY: (*Concerned.*) Police?

CHARLIE: Yeah, I went down the bookies, when I come back... ah, they jus' turned things over a bit. Nothin' serious, room was back to normal in a few minutes.

JENNY: Aint you heard about all them burglaries? They locked that granny in her bedroom, nearly starved her to death. No, Charlie, you're comin' wi' me. We'll have a quickie down the club, then I'll get us some dinner, yeah?

CHARLIE: Well...

JENNY: Come on.

CHARLIE: Alright then, just for tonight.

Exit JENNY and CHARLIE.

Momentarily CHARLIE enters in a hurry. He quickly finds a hat and tries it on for size. He is somewhat mindful and moves to his hiding place and retrieves the paperwork. He dials a number on the telephone.

Hello, Duke? Charlie. (*Beat.*) You've waited twenty years, I'm sure another five minutes won't hurt...

Yeah, got 'em right here. They make for some pretty interestin' readings. Thing is, Duke, they don't come cheap... (*Pause.*) Well, tomorrow's as good a time as any...

JENNY enters.

JENNY: Charlie, you coming, or what – ? (*Seeing CHARLIE on telephone.*) Oh...

CHARLIE: So tomorrow, then. Yeah, bye.

CHARLIE hangs up the receiver and attempts to conceal the paperwork behind his back. JENNY senses the uneasy atmosphere.

JENNY: You ready then?

CHARLIE: Just a minute...

CHARLIE grabs the hat and places it on his head. He turns to JENNY.

How do I look?

JENNY: You look great. Can we go now?

JENNY exits.

CHARLIE breathes a huge sigh of relief, then stuffs the paperwork in his clothing and exits.

Fade down lights.

Scene 3

Lights fade up. Enter LUKE. He is anxious, uncertain as he peers out the window. He plugs in and begins playing his computer game. The doorbell rings. LUKE stops for a moment. When he's sure whoever it is has gone he returns to the game. Momentarily his mobile telephone rings. He looks at it but ultimately doesn't answer it.

LUKE: Tchoh, man. Stop botherin' me. Jus' leave me
alone. You're makin' me vex.

This sets him off in an impromptu rap.

You're just vexing me
Hexing me
Ringing my mobile
Texting me
You don't know my game?
Now you're perplexing me
I know its rough out there
Tough out there
Armageddon's in the atmosphere
Man an man's on a huff out there
Wanna puff out there
Turn a nice dream into your worst nightmare
But you're goin' on rash – brash
Wanna give me the lash – mash
Over a little hash – stash
All I wanted was to dash, cash
Nice garms, nice treads
lookin' flash at th' bash
So you're sayin' I'm whack – Cack
But I'm ahead of the pack – Black
Ghetto soldier fightin' back – Attack
Wanna gimme the sack? – Quack!
And now you wanna come with it
Run with it
Let it go blood,
just done with it
You gonna serve me a writ?
Hear what, I quit
Not tomorrow, today idiot
You must see it as I see it
Done my bit, now I'm going legit
Aint chatting crap or gobbledy gook
So don't come to me with no rebuke
You're making me sick, man, makin' me puke?

What am I?
Some kind of mook?
No bredrens, I'm the duke
Mic master MC Luke

Lights fade down.

End of Act One.

ACT TWO

Scene 1

Lights fade up. It's raining heavily outside. Enter JENNY and CHARLIE, taking off wet coats.

JENNY: Bleedin' hell, it's really coming down today.

CHARLIE: Good old England, ya can't beat it.

CHARLIE hands JENNY a towel, then exits.

She dampens down her hair and wipes her face dry.

CHARLIE: (*Off.*) Two sugars aint it?

JENNY: One these days, Charlie. I'm tryin' to cut down, tryin' to eat more healthy. Two pieces of fruit a day we're s'posed to eat. An' we're s'posed to drink eight glasses of water. Them bloody scientists aint seen the colour of that river.

Enter CHARLIE with two mugs of tea.

CHARLIE: There you go, love.

JENNY: Cheers.(*Takes a sip.*) Bloody good job I bumped into you. I woulda' got soaked. Let me guess, you went down the bookies, right? Ask me where I been?

CHARLIE: Go on, where you been?

JENNY: I got up this mornin' an' I thought dammit, I'm gonna do it, I am.

CHARLIE: What?

JENNY: It's been such a long time. I had a real job digging out all the papers, but I did it. I went and re-registered, didn't I. I'm gonna finish my course.

CHARLIE: That's cracking news.

JENNY: Of course it's all changed now, all these new regulations an' that, but I thought, 'Do it now, Jenny.'

CHARLIE: No time like the present.

JENNY: Chose a terrible day for it though, in all this rain.

CHARLIE: They say rain like that is the only thing that keeps the rat population in check. Floods the sewers, see, drowns whole generations of the buggers. Watchin' them people run for shelter, seems like the rain's also tryin' to wash the filth away on top.

JENNY: God's unhappy, that's what my mum used to say.

CHARLIE: Take a good look down here, you can't blame him.

JENNY: Yeah, but I bet it takes more than God cryin' to stop you playin' the tote, eh Charlie?

CHARLIE: Yeah, you got it.

JENNY takes a sip from her tea.

JENNY: Best drink of the day, tea.

CHARLIE: Yeah. (*Beat.*) I er, stopped off for a bit on the way back.

JENNY: Eh?

CHARLIE: Went over the water. Been to see an old friend I aint seen in a while.

JENNY: Good on you, Charlie. You an' them geezers used to be out all the time, boxing, football, racing.

CHARLIE: Not wrong there.

JENNY: I was sayin' that to Alex at Millie's memorial the other day, that you should get out more, see your old friends again.

CHARLIE: Did ya?

JENNY: Yeah. He cut me dead.

CHARLIE: That's my boy.

JENNY: Let's not beat around the bush. I mean, he's your only child, an' he leaves you down here... No disrespect, Charlie, but you're livin' in...

CHARLIE: None taken, Jenny.

JENNY: You know what I mean. Him livin' out there in the suburbs like you don't exist. You hear what he was sayin'?

CHARLIE: I heard.

JENNY: Sayin' how you ruined his life, got him the sack an' everythin'.

CHARLIE: Well I did in a way...

JENNY: As far as I remember, that weren't down to you. He left that job of his own accord.

CHARLIE: Yeah...

JENNY: I mean, come on.

CHARLIE: He was seventeen when that letter come through the door, Metropolitan Police stamped all over it. I thought, 'What now, what's he done?' Then I find out it's an application form. Did I give him some stick for that.

JENNY: Damn right, too, joining the old bill behind your back like that. He's gotta learn to live by his own actions.

CHARLIE: He loved them cop shows when he was a kid... you know the ones where the villains always get done.

JENNY: It's not real life though, is it?

CHARLIE: It was for him, til my oar went in an' tipped it all arse over tit.

JENNY: There's no excuse for goin' on like that at his mum's memorial. She'll be turnin' in her grave, she will. God rest her soul.

CHARLIE: Aah, he wasn't the only one had a drop too much.

JENNY: Drop too much? He was rat-arsed, Charlie, in front of all them people. Excuse my French, but it was fuckin' disgraceful, it was. He's got a real problem, he has.

CHARLIE: He's not all to blame.

JENNY: I know you two don't see eye to eye, but if Luke ever did that to me…

CHARLIE: Aah, you just get on with it, don't ya. Let sleepin' dogs lie.

JENNY: Stubborn git.

JENNY is slightly embarrassed at her frankness.

Anyway, you shouldn't have to deal with all that at your age…an' all these bloody hooligans forcin' us behind doors twenty-four seven.

CHARLIE: Yeah, that's what it is these days.

JENNY: It's the old ones I feel sorry for.

CHARLIE: Pass sixty-five, you're no use to society, you're forgotten, don't exist no more. They chuck you in jail, toss away the key.

JENNY: An' the bloody police are doing sweet FA about it.

The doorbell rings.

I'll get it.

CHARLIE: Leave it, it's just them bloody kids windin' me up. They been at it all week.

JENNY: D'you know who it is? We go down the council, they'll evict them.

CHARLIE: Luke reckons it's the little albino kid from down th' road.

JENNY: Dundus? Lorraine Archer's boy? That little kid's out of order. Wait til I see her.

The doorbell rings again, this time more vigorously.

NELSON: (*Off.*) Oi, Charlie! Charlie, open the door.

JENNY: Who's that?

CHARLIE: What does he want?

CHARLIE exits, momentarily returning with NELSON.

NELSON: I'm lookin' for Luke.

JENNY: He's not 'ere.

CHARLIE: I told him.

NELSON: I been lookin' everywhere for him. Been ringin' him as well, but the man don't answer his friggin' mobile.

JENNY: We only just got here ourselves.

NELSON: I'll wait, yeah?

CHARLIE: Well, it's a bit inconvenient, right now. I'm havin' a bit of a natter with a friend.

NELSON: It's alright, you can natter. I'll wait.

CHARLIE: When I see Luke I'll tell him you were here lookin' for him.

NELSON: I'll wait.

There's a pause, uncomfortable.

JENNY: Are you Greg?

NELSON: Greg, who's that?

JENNY: Luke's friend.

NELSON: I'm his friend.

JENNY: Which friend?

NELSON: Not Greg, you get me.

JENNY: Who are you, then?

NELSON: You don't know me?

JENNY: If I did, I wouldn't ask, would I?

NELSON laughs.

So come on?

NELSON: You musta' heard of me, I'm Nelson.

JENNY: Nelson, I never heard of no Nelson.

NELSON: He never mention me?

JENNY: No. I'd remember if he did.

NELSON: Well, me an' him is friend, believe.

There's a pause as tension grows.

JENNY: You got a black car, aint ya?

NELSON: You do know me.

JENNY: I've seen you drivin' about in that car.

NELSON: That's a luxury motor, you know.

JENNY: I look like I care?

NELSON: Thirty-eight grand's worth of stainless steel car, you get me.

JENNY: So what you doing drivin' a car like that round 'ere?

NELSON: Hey sister, you don't see it? Day in, day out, all the ghetto youths is just gettin' lick down all the time, on telly, radio, papers, on street. I want them to see that they too can lock on a nice chops, wear nice garms an' drive a nice motor. I want them young bloods to see that they can reach the top, you get me.

CHARLIE: (*Sneering.*) The top?

NELSON: I suppose you wanna go for a ride, yeah?

JENNY kisses her teeth and turns away.

NELSON laughs.

JENNY: You don't even live round 'ere much less.

NELSON: How you mean? I grow round 'ere, this is my hood. Check with Charlie, he knows the runnings.

CHARLIE: From over the other side of the estate, Jenny, the old block.

JENNY: Where they knock down that school to build a shopping centre?

CHARLIE: You got it.

NELSON: F'real. This estate is my manor.

Another pause.

JENNY: A bit old, aint ya, to be hangin' about with a fifteen year old?

NELSON: I got experience, ennit.

JENNY: Well, he needs to grow up in his own time.

71

NELSON: The youth grow without a father.

JENNY: And?

NELSON: He have to learn how to be a man, still.

JENNY: Anything he needs to learn, he can learn it from me.

NELSON: (*Laughing.*) From you? No man, from what I hear, he don't like the man about your house. That's where I come in.

CHARLIE: Hold it, I think we'll stop right there.

NELSON: Hear what, he never tell me he had a strong Nubian woman for his mother.

JENNY: (*Sneering.*) Yeah, that's right.

NELSON: Well I like the way you carry yourself, the way you jus' sexy.

JENNY: Get lost.

NELSON: Ennit Charlie? The woman tight, fit an' sexy, criss like a biscuit!

NELSON sits on the sofa and begins playing the computer game.

There is another tension building pause before he suddenly discards the game.

What them kids see in this rubbish? Charlie, how about some tea?

CHARLIE: I'm outa' milk.

NELSON: But you English love tea, though, ennit?

CHARLIE: You been up to see your dad?

NELSON: No, I can't, the man blubberin' an' shit, no.

CHARLIE: He asks after you.

NELSON: Yeah?

CHARLIE: What can I say, he thinks you play cricket.

NELSON: Idiot.

JENNY: You disrespect your father like that?

NELSON: (*Harshly.*) That aint my father. My father was a fighter.

JENNY: I was you I'd feel shame.

NELSON: I can't even look at the man. He aint sick, he's a coward.

CHARLIE: You got some nerve. Sit down here ridin' around in your poncey chariot an' you wanna talk about coward?

NELSON: (*Indignant.*) Not many of us ever get a chance like what he had. (*Beat.*) We waited for him to come home...two days, two weeks, two months. It was ten years before I see him again, walkin' street with his arse hangin' out. I got people pointin' at me, 'Look, the Cock's son, ha ha ha.' You know how many man I had to carve up?

CHARLIE: Took bravery to do what he did.

NELSON: What, walk out on his missus an' kids?

CHARLIE: That was...

NELSON: He left her strugglin' with four kids an nothin' but hungry belly. He pussied out, man, an' I watched my mum fall apart. What goes around comes around? I don't know how you can back him up anyway, Charlie? He cost you an' your bredrens much cash. I heard it was well over a million.

JENNY: A million?

NELSON: Yeah, way back when that was nuff corn.

JENNY: Cor, they can half gossip round 'ere. That aint right is it, Charlie?

NELSON: (*Beat.*) You don't know about it, ennit? Go on, Charlie, tell her. Tell the woman how you an' your friends destroyed my family. Why you think his own son dissed him?

JENNY: Charlie...?

CHARLIE: (*Pause.*) You know me, I was always interested in the fight game. Anyway me an' three mates thought we might get us a fighter. I knew his dad, used to see him fight down the town hall. He was fit, tough, had a good jaw. He had great potential, coulda' gone all the way. So we got together in a consortium to manage his career. (*Beat.*) Three fights in, three times he struggles to make the weight. Alarm bells. We find out too late he's got a taste for the good life, birds, booze, clubs. It was a real job to get him in the gym, he hated trainin'. Seventy-five grand we'd laid out. Saw that goin' down the swanney, so we hatch a plan to recoup our investment. We put him in the ring against a chinny has-been, Johnny Carver. He was supposed to go down in round six.

JENNY: You mean, he was gonna take a dive?

NELSON: Alright, you see it now!

CHARLIE: Bets go on all over the country, ten to one against. We stood to make more than two million.

NELSON: Two million! An' I bet all you was gonna give him was a cuppa tea an' a fuckin' doughnut. But hear what, this time for once in his life he stood up like a man. Round six, he lost on points. Round seven,

Carver takes a standin' eight. Next round he showed the
world that what a white man can do, a black man can
do better. He knocked that fucker out, broke his jaw.

CHARLIE: It was pandemonium at ringside, fuses goin'
out all around me. I thought, that's it, he's dead, he's a
dead man.

NELSON: They lose their money that night.

CHARLIE: The boxing board an' the old bill got wind of
it, started sniffin' around, askin' questions. Even my boy,
Alex got suspicious.

NELSON: Everybody was searchin' for my old man… my
mum, gangsters, police. It was like he just disappeared
off the face of the earth. But all the time he was here,
right here.

JENNY: Here?

CHARLIE: Here.

JENNY: So let me get this, you bring a big big black man
to come live in your house with you an' your wife?

CHARLIE: You can imagine, Millie weren't very happy
about it.

JENNY: You don't say.

CHARLIE: But you know her Jenny, bend over backwards
for anyone in trouble. She saw him as just a mate down
on his luck.

JENNY: God rest her soul.

NELSON: I lost respect for him the day he let white man's
pride put him in the funny farm. (*Changing tack.*) Hey,
I never come here to chat about me. I got business,
dread. This youth is causin' me nuff stress. Look how
long I been 'ere already.

CHARLIE: To be honest, Horatio, I don't really see any point in you waitin'. When Luke comes I'll tell him –

NELSON leaps to his feet in an explosion of anger.

NELSON: Hey, what did I tell you about that raas name? What's my name? What do they call me?

JENNY: Oh my God!

NELSON: My name old man!

CHARLIE: Nelson, that's your name, Nelson.

NELSON: Yeah, that's better.

There's a short pause, then NELSON laughs. He bounces round the room mimicking Mohammed Ali boxing, his famous shuffle.

(*Singing.*) 'Mohammed, Mohammed Ali
Float like a butterfly an' sting like a bee…'
(*Mimicking.*) 'What's my name? Ali… say my name…
Ali.' Remember that…Ali, Floyd Patterson?

JENNY: I hate boxing.

NELSON: This aint about boxing. It's about survival.

JENNY: What, two black men beating the living shit out of each other?

NELSON: The man refuse to go down. That was pride, you get me. Patterson got a batterin' that night.

CHARLIE: Yeah.

NELSON: That was some fight, ennit?

CHARLIE: It was a good fight.

NELSON: How you mean good fight? It was a bad fight! It was wicked!

NELSON calms down, getting back to business.

(*Beat.*) So what, he never said nothin'?

CHARLIE: Who?

NELSON: I'm talkin' to the woman.

JENNY: I got a name.

NELSON: Whatever it is, you know where Luke is?

JENNY: No.

NELSON: I went round his house an' he aint there neither.

JENNY: Listen, I don't want people like you comin' round my house.

NELSON: Tchoh! I been in there already. Plenty times.

JENNY: That boy...

NELSON: I don't wanna have to go round everywhere lookin' for him, you knaa'. I'm already gettin' didgy, you get me.

JENNY: What d'you want with him anyway?

NELSON: Business.

JENNY: What business?

NELSON: My business.

JENNY: Your business? What business you got with my son?

NELSON: I didn't jus' tell you it's my business?

JENNY: Well, he aint around, he's busy.

NELSON: Busy?

JENNY: Yeah busy. He works. In a shop.

NELSON: (*Laughing.*) Work? Shop? He done with that Ghandi-man, Khan from long time.

JENNY: What?

NELSON: You never know?

NELSON laughs.

JENNY: (*Confused.*) He was…he had a paper round…he had money, Charlie?

CHARLIE: It's true.

JENNY: You knew?

CHARLIE: Well, I thought he was up to somethin' and…

JENNY: You thought he was up to somethin' an' you couldn't tell me?

CHARLIE: I had to make sure.

JENNY: You had to make sure? He's my son, Charlie!

CHARLIE: Jenny, I didn't wanna worry you. I thought I could…

JENNY: Thought you could what, thought you could what?

NELSON laughs again.

NELSON: Go on, Charlie, tell th' woman.

CHARLIE: I had a word with him…

JENNY: (*Stressing the words.*) And what was it he was up to?

CHARLIE: (*Pointing to NELSON.*) Ask him.

NELSON: Ask him yourself when you see him.

JENNY: (*To NELSON.*) God, I hate people like you.

NELSON: Tchoh! You don't even know me.

JENNY: Thank the lord for small mercies.

NELSON: The Lord can't help you. But hear what, sexy thing like you, behave yourself, you can make some proper corn out there.

JENNY: Piss off.

NELSON: One of my bredrens control the scene. I can help you.

JENNY: There's nothin' I want from you.

NELSON: (*Smirking.*) Them jeans, your boy buy them for you, ennit?

There's a slight pause. Then JENNY leaps up and begins removing her jeans.

JENNY: You lot round come round 'ere... you're scum...

CHARLIE: Jenny, what you doin'?

JENNY: (*Continuing.*) You're like a disease, a cancer. You take set, then you grow an' grow til you destroy everythin'...

JENNY tosses her jeans at NELSON.

JENNY: Here, these are yours!

NELSON: An' the rest, take off the rest!

JENNY: These I bought with my money!

NELSON: (*Excitedly.*) I don't care, take it off! All of it, take it all off!

JENNY: I aint scared of you.

CHARLIE tries to intervene.

CHARLIE: Jenny...

JENNY: Move from me, Charlie

NELSON: Show me everythin'. I wan' see you naked to the day you born.

JENNY: Yeah, come on then, you wanker!

JENNY removes her blouse and tosses it at NELSON who mimes a Jamaican dancehall routine with a cigarette lighter and a gun.

NELSON: Let me see it, I wan' see it. Lord o' Mercy! Flash me lighter! Bow, bow, bow!

JENNY: You want more... More?

CHARLIE: Jenny, that's it, this is crazy!

CHARLIE pushes JENNY aside and turns to NELSON.

Now you listen to me, Lord fuckin' Horatio Nelson, whatever you wanna call yourself...the clock's ticking, your days round 'ere are numbered. So if I was you I'd make myself scarce. I'd go, now!

NELSON: What's this, what's goin' on here? Everybody fuckin' with me today! (*To JENNY.*) Your son fuckin' with me, you fuckin' with me, an' now Charlie!

NELSON turns and moves threateningly towards CHARLIE.

Talk to me them way there? You aint even on my level. You don't know me. Nobody talk to me like that. I'm gonna teach you the meanin' of respect...

NELSON grabs CHARLIE round the throat and pulls a knife from his pocket.

CHARLIE: No, no...

JENNY: Charlie...!

NELSON: Your day done, old man! New generation!

Suddenly LUKE bursts from the bedroom.

LUKE: (*Yelling.*) No. Stop it, stop it, stop it!

Everybody freezes, there's a pause.

JENNY: Luke...

NELSON: You was here all this time?

JENNY: Luke, what's goin' on?

NELSON: You have my t'ings right?

JENNY: Luke...

CHARLIE: Jenny, wait.

JENNY: No, I wanna know what this idiot's been up to. Come on?

LUKE: I think I'm in trouble.

NELSON: I ask you for my things?

JENNY: Someone tell me what's goin' on!

LUKE: It aint there. It was in the settee. But it's gone.

NELSON: Gone?

LUKE: Someone took it.

NELSON: You lose my business! (*Shaking his head.*) Luke, Luke, Luke, Luke...

LUKE: I worked it out though. If we explain about the break-ins an' everythin'...your people, they know everyone, yeah, they can use their contacts to find out who's been doin' it. Then they can get their stuff back. Whaddya' think?

NELSON: (*Beat.*) Come, let's go.

JENNY: Luke, no...

JENNY grabs hold of LUKE.

You aint goin' nowhere.

LUKE: It's alright, mum, it's safe. I'll be back soon.

CHARLIE: Nelson, I'll give you five hundred quid.

NELSON pauses.

A thousand?

NELSON laughs as he exits with LUKE.

JENNY is hysterical.

JENNY: He's taken him, Charlie, where's he takin' him?

CHARLIE: I don't know.

JENNY: Do something!

CHARLIE: Jenny, wait.

JENNY: Charlie what we gonna do?

CHARLIE: I'm thinkin'.

JENNY: The police, I'll call the police.

CHARLIE: No.

JENNY: We have to.

CHARLIE: We don't want them involved.

JENNY: He took him away an' you did nothin', I'm callin' the police.

JENNY dials on the phone.

Hello, police…

CHARLIE hangs up the phone.

What're you doin'?

CHARLIE: I told ya, we don't want them involved.

JENNY: He's gonna hurt my son!

CHARLIE: He won't.

JENNY: He will.

CHARLIE: He won't hurt him, Jenny.

JENNY: You don't know?

CHARLIE: I know.

JENNY: I don't care what you know, I'm callin' the police.

CHARLIE: Jenny, how long have you known me? Trust me on this one, alright. I already made my move.

JENNY: What move? Charlie, what have you done?

CHARLIE: I've arranged things. I've straightened everythin' out. Luke's gonna be fine.

JENNY: He's gonna be fine?

CHARLIE: After today, he'll have no more trouble, he'll be in the clear. Then its up to him, whichever way he wants to go. Everyone deserves one chance, Jenny... everyone deserves a chance.

A police siren is heard.

Fade down lights.

Scene 2

Fade up lights.

CHARLIE flicks through a newspaper. LUKE's right arm is encased in a plaster cast and he plays his computer game in a somewhat frustrated manner.

LUKE: Come on, come on, bloody hell!

CHARLIE: Oi.

LUKE: I was gettin' to level five before. Now I can't even get off the first one.

CHARLIE: You will soon enough.

LUKE discards the game in frustration.

LUKE: I can't do nothin', man. I can't play football, can't ride my bike. I'm so so bored.

CHARLIE: And whose fault's that?

LUKE: I feel like a freak with this thing on my hand, can't even go out with my girl.

CHARLIE: (*Beat.*) What girl's that then?

LUKE: Jansheera, ennit.

CHARLIE: Jansheera, Mr Khan's daughter?

LUKE: Know that. She's sweet, man. I chirpsed her when she was in my science class.

CHARLIE: I don't see her ringin' you on that mobile phone of yours.

LUKE: We fell out, ennit. She said I left her dad in the lurch. She blanked me, you know…right in front of my boys, which was proper out of order, you get me. Comin' to me with them attitudes there, I did run her, mate, told her about herself.

CHARLIE: Oh, yeah?

LUKE: Yeah. But don't worry about it though, Charlie, it's all good still.

CHARLIE: It is, is it?

LUKE: Believe. Cos once this thing's off, mate, I got nuff making up to do, trust me.

CHARLIE: I can see that. You're right handed, aint ya?

CHARLIE indicates LUKE's injured arm.

LUKE: Yeah, yeah very funny.

CHARLIE: Well, I hope now you learnt your lesson.

LUKE: What lesson?

CHARLIE: You know what I'm talking about.

LUKE: Alright, Charlie. (*Pause.*) Six months in traction. They said he's lucky to be alive.

CHARLIE: Nasty bit of luck that.

LUKE: The Feds reckon it was a joyrider.

CHARLIE: Enough of them round here.

LUKE: They still aint found the car or the driver.

CHARLIE: They'll find that car burnt out somewhere.

LUKE: I don't think so.

CHARLIE: What's that?

LUKE: It weren't no joyrider.

CHARLIE: Whaddya mean?

LUKE: That weren't no joyrider.

CHARLIE: The police know this type of thing. If they say it's a joyrider then that's what it is.

LUKE: I saw the car.

CHARLIE: I should think so. It hit you, didn't it?

LUKE: It was parked up by the kebab shop. One of them old BMs, the square one, double parked it was.

CHARLIE: Oh yeah?

LUKE: I remember, we was walkin' past the post office. We get to the zebra crossing an' as we go to cross the road, this car just speeds up. It was drivin' straight at us.

CHARLIE: You sure?

LUKE: The driver had this Nike baseball cap on, an' wraparound sunglasses. I can still see him in my mind, it was like some mad dream. I jumped back, yeah, an' I fell over. Then I see Nelson… he was up in the air. He looked like a rag doll, arms an' legs all over the shop. He dropped an' bounced in the road. He was all twisted up, I thought he was dead. Then I look up an' the car was gone, an' this lady was screamin', an' my arm was hurtin'. I saw it, Charlie. It was like…like he was waitin' for us.

CHARLIE: That's shock, that is. It does that sometimes, makes people see things that didn't actually happen. You stepped out in the road without lookin' is what you did.

LUKE: No, man, I saw it. It weren't no joyrider, Charlie. Whoever it was, was out to get us. Dennis said Nelson musta' owed someone an' it was payback time.

CHARLIE: Dennis, what does he know?

LUKE: He come down the hospital. Gave me a right bollockin'. Sayin' how I dissed my mum an' how I was lucky I only got a broken arm.

CHARLIE: He's right.

LUKE: I never dissed my mum.

CHARLIE: You lied to her.

LUKE: I never lied to her.

CHARLIE: You lived a lie, Luke. You weren't only lying to her an' everybody else, you were lyin' to yourself.

There's a seething pause.

LUKE: An' what about you?

CHARLIE: Me?

LUKE: What about all the things you done?

CHARLIE: This aint about me.

LUKE: Aint it? Goin' on all stoosh like you're somebody, always lecturing me like I'm one of them idiot boys you see walking road.

CHARLIE: (*Laughing nervously.*) You're a one, aint ya?

LUKE: Just hold it down, blood, yeah. Come givin' it the big 'un... you can't say nothin' to me, mate.

CHARLIE: What?

LUKE: Yeah, that's right. I know what it is round 'ere. You aint the only one with his nose to the ground, you get me.

CHARLIE: You got somethin' you wanna say to me?

LUKE: When I'm ready.

CHARLIE: When you're ready?

LUKE: Yeah, when I'm ready.

CHARLIE: When's that then?

LUKE: You wanna let it go, Charlie, yeah. Cos right now, I'm like a timebomb waitin' to go off, you get me. Yeah, like a volcano jus' waitin' to erupt in the house...

CHARLIE laughs, somewhat nervously, then falls serious.

CHARLIE: (*Beat.*) You ever hear the sayin', what goes around comes around? Well, play Knock Down Ginger enough times you'll find yourself knockin' on your own front door.

LUKE: What?

CHARLIE: You heard.

LUKE: What's that shit mean?

CHARLIE: It means my past stays where it is.

LUKE: What, like taxing people, then torturing them and burnin' 'em down cos they won't pay up... robbing jewelery shops an' cigarette factories, ringin' cars, illegal gamblin', fraud? What's all that, then, eh?

There's a pause.

CHARLIE: I told you I weren't no angel.

LUKE: Yeah, that copper, Chisholm told me, told me everything. He said the only thing stopped you from goin' jail was when Alex nicked your police files. He's your son an' he gave up his career for you. So don't come the high an' fuckin' mighty with me.

CHARLIE: I'll tell you somethin' else, shall I, little big man? Your mate, Nelson lyin' in that hospital is fit for only two things, the nick or the cemetery.

LUKE: Stay outa' what don't concern you. You think you know everythin'.

CHARLIE: That piece of shit is small fry. Just one more word from me an' it's 'bye bye'.

CHARLIE draws his hand across his throat.

LUKE: (*Realisation.*) That...that was you? You done it? He nearly got killed.

CHARLIE: That's the thing with bad lads, you can't trust 'em to do a job properly.

LUKE: That could be me in that hospital.

CHARLIE: Thank your lucky stars it aint.

LUKE: I coulda' got killed.

CHARLIE: But you didn't.

LUKE: I could've, though.

CHARLIE: Yeah, you could've. But you didn't.

LUKE: What's wrong with you?

CHARLIE: (*Pointedly.*) I had those fuckin' files nearly twenty years. Worth their weight in gold they were. An' to save your stupid arse, I give 'em away for nothin'... Nothin'!

LUKE explodes in a rage.

LUKE: Well, fuck you then! I come round 'ere, help you out... I aint comin' round 'ere no more. (*Beat.*) Think you're somethin' special... You're a lonely old twat who smells an' lives in shit, that's what they say about you round 'ere? Dirty fuckin' paedophile nonce!

LUKE pushes over the newspaper pile and a chair and exits.

CHARLIE is stunned. He moves around the room somewhat in a daze, sighing heavily and finally burying his head in his hands.

Momentarily LUKE reappears, somewhat sheepishly.

CHARLIE turns when he sees him.

CHARLIE: Luke?

LUKE: What I said, those things... I never...

CHARLIE: Sometimes people say a lot of things when they're angry. An' sometimes they do things the wrong way too. But deep down you always know that it's because they care what happens to ya.

They hug, somewhat awkwardly, but well-meaning.

LUKE: (*Pause.*) You know what I'm gonna do? I'm gonna get rid of all these old newspapers.

LUKE begins gathering up the newspapers.

CHARLIE: Oi, I aint finished reading 'em.

LUKE: Come on, Charlie, you'll never get round to it...
especially when I get my paper round back. I'll bring
you a new one every day.

CHARLIE: I don't want any more of them Suns, Mirrors
or Expresses. Get me one of them broadsheets, The
Times, or the Guardian...

LUKE: The big papers? You'll never get through 'em.

CHARLIE: You're gettin' there, son, you're gettin' there.

The doorbell rings.

They both look round.

Fade down lights.

The End.